RC 89- 93

W9-CFI-069

When You Go To
KINDERGARTEN

▲ Text by James Howe

■ Photographs by Betsy Imershein

Alfred A. Knopf

New York

This is a Borzoi Book published by Alfred A. Knopf, Inc.

Text copyright © 1986 by James Howe
Illustrations copyright © 1986 by Betsy Imershein
All rights reserved under International and Pan-American Copyright
Conventions. Published in the United States by Alfred A. Knopf, Inc.,
New York, and simultaneously in Canada by Random House of
Canada Limited, Toronto. Distributed by Random House, Inc., New York.
Manufactured in the United States of America
2   4   6   8   0   9   7   5   3   1

Library of Congress Cataloging-in-Publication Data
Howe, James. When you go to kindergarten.
Summary: Text and photographs explain what it is like to
go to kindergarten.
1. Kindergarten—Juvenile literature. [1. Kindergarten.
2. Schools] I. Imershein, Betsy, ill. II. Title.
LB1169.H58   1985   372'.218   85-18055
ISBN 0-394-87303-3   ISBN 0-394-97303-8 (lib. bdg.)

We are indebted to the principals, teachers, children, parents, and staff of three
schools who were especially generous with themselves and their time. Our special
thanks to Dr. Sheila Terens, Frank Small, Martha Michaels, Priscilla Caine, Ronnie
Shulman, Barbara Gold, Gail Pugliese, and Florence Cohn, Number Four School,
Inwood, New York; Sandra Roche and Cleo Banks, Little Red Schoolhouse, New
York, New York; and Dr. Ellin Carpenter and Vic Klein, Bryant School, Teaneck,
New Jersey.

We also wish to thank Shirley Gagliano, Franklin Elementary School, Hewlett,
New York; Lee Howe, Nancy Beatty, Sylvia Rowe, Claire Blanton, and Maxine
Rosen, Allen Creek School, Pittsford, New York; Georgie Bramley, Park Road
School, Pittsford, New York; Peg Bridges, Thornell School, Pittsford, New York;
Dr. Leslie Williams, Dr. James Borland, and Andrea VanHoven, Teachers College,
Columbia University; Dr. Selma Knobler, Bank Street College; Dr. Doris Fromberg,
Hofstra University; Janet F. Brown and Felicia George, National Association for the
Education of Young Children; Susan Howe, Lois Imershein, Nancy Carver, and
Adam Carver; and our editors, Dinah Stevenson and Stephanie Spinner, our art
director, Denise Cronin, and our designer, Eileen Rosenthal, for their help.

By sharing their insights and experiences and allowing themselves to be observed
and photographed, many people, named and unnamed, assisted in the creation of
this book. We are grateful to them all.

With love to
Lois and Charles Imershein

Introduction for Parents

Going to kindergarten is a unique experience in the life of any child, even a child who has been to day care or nursery school. In the eyes of most children, kindergarten is "the big school," and entering the big school represents a giant step in growing up. This book is designed to help your child take that step with enthusiasm and a sense of pride.

When You Go To Kindergarten presents a variety of schools, children, and teachers, rather than looking at one school or at one child's experience. As you and your child read the book together, your child will undoubtedly have specific questions about what his or her school experience will be like. You may well want to discuss the differences between what is written or shown here and what you know your child's situation will be.

Sharing this book can be especially valuable before your child starts kindergarten, when he or she is curious about the new situation and may be feeling some anxiety. But there may be times throughout the school year when you'll want to go through the book as well, addressing new questions your child may have and reliving new experiences together.

Your child will take the step into "the big school" more easily if he or she is prepared and is given support and understanding. Still, letting go of a small hand can be as hard on you as it is on your child. Just remember that when you let go of that hand, you are allowing your child to take hold of something even greater—a sense of himself or herself in the world.

Starting kindergarten is an exciting part of growing up. You will be going to a new place, making new friends, having fun, and learning—all at the same time! If you've been to nursery school or day care, you know what it's like to spend time away from home. But kindergarten isn't the same as nursery school or day care. This book will tell you about kindergarten—and what it's like to go there.

How will you get to school? If you live nearby, you might walk. A grownup you know well, such as your mother or father, an older brother or sister, or a baby sitter, will walk with you. And crossing or safety patrol guards will be at the street corners to help you safely across.

If you live farther away from the school, you might
go in a car. But you will probably ride in a big yellow
bus with other children going to the same school.
The bus will pick you up every school day at a bus
stop near your home. The bus driver will take you to
school and bring you home when school is over.

Your going to school is
something for you and your
parents to feel good about,
even though it may be hard
to say good-bye at first.

Your teacher will be at the school to meet you when
you come to kindergarten the first day and every day.

Your school may be a very big place with long halls. Some schools have stairs. Some have many classrooms and special rooms such as a library, a gymnasium, and an auditorium. Most schools have a principal's office and a nurse's office.

Your school may also seem big at first because it is a strange, new place and there may be many boys and girls older and bigger than you. It won't be strange for long, however. Soon you will know your way around, and then the school will no longer seem so big. If you should get lost, there are many adults—teachers and custodians, for instance—who can help you find your way back to your classroom.

Most of your time in kindergarten will be spent in your classroom. Here there are tables and chairs just your size, as well as pictures on the walls, books to look at, and all sorts of things for you to work and play with every day.

On the first day you'll meet the other children who will be in your kindergarten class with you. They're all starting out—just like you.

Name tags will help everyone learn each other's names.

In some schools the bathrooms are in the hall outside the classroom. Your teacher will show you where they are and how to tell which is the girls' bathroom and which is the boys'. There are also water fountains in the hall.

In some schools the bathroom is right in the classroom. There will be a door you can close and, whether the bathroom is inside your classroom or outside, you will be able to use it whenever you need to.

Each day when you get
to your room you will hang
up your outdoor clothes,
put your belongings in a
special place . . .

and spend a little quiet time looking at books or
playing.

Soon your teacher will ask everyone to sit down together and start the day by taking attendance. "Taking attendance" means finding out who is in school and who is absent. While you're sitting together, you might also talk about what the teacher has planned for you to do that day.

Then you might stand to say the Pledge of Allegiance to the flag. Everyone will say the pledge together. The teacher will help those children who don't know all the words.

Your teacher will also help everyone learn the rules of being together as a group. When you are working, when you are playing, when you are doing most of the things you will do every day in school, it is important to . . .

share . . .

listen and not
talk while others
are talking . . .

raise your hand
to ask a question or
give an answer . . .

get in line . . . and
take turns.

From the first day of
kindergarten in the fall to the
last day in the spring, you
will have lots to do that is
fun and interesting.

You'll learn new things
about numbers and counting.

You'll learn about the alphabet. Your teacher will
help you learn to print your letters and to hear the
sounds that the letters make.

He or she will help you get ready to read by
reading stories to the whole class.

And there will be books with pictures that you can look at by yourself.

Some children do not know how to read when they are in kindergarten. Other children do know how. This doesn't mean that they are better or smarter. It just means that they are ready to read sooner. Everybody reads whenever he or she is ready.

You'll learn about colors and shapes and sizes . . .

and animals and plants.

You'll sing songs . . .

paint pictures . . .

and make things.

You'll build with blocks . . .

and play make-believe.

Sometimes you'll go outside to learn . . .

and sometimes to play.

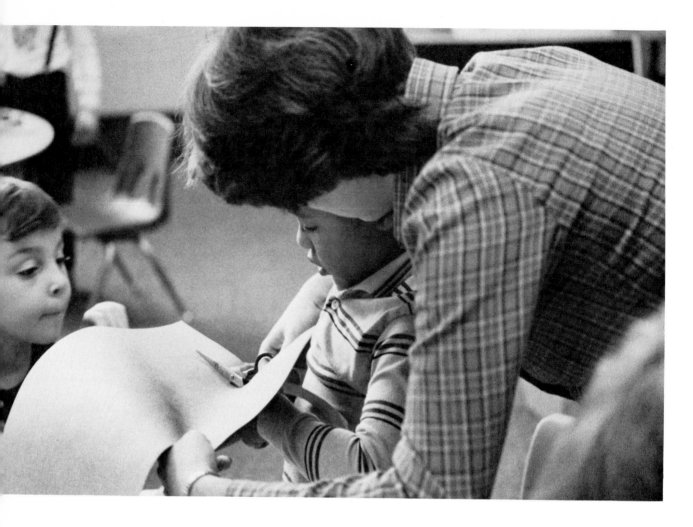

It's fun to learn new things. And your teacher will always be there to help you.

There will be times when you can help the teacher, too. He or she will let you know how you can help. One way is to clean up after working or playing.

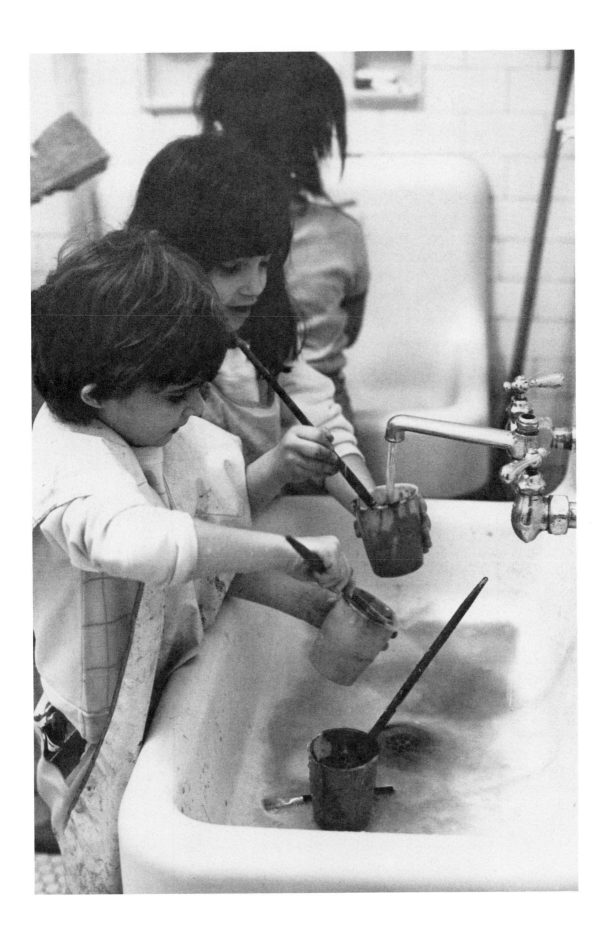

You will have something to eat—a snack or lunch—
every day at school.

One important thing that happens in school a few times every year is a fire drill. A fire drill is a way of practicing what to do and where to go in case there is a fire in your school building. You will hear a loud bell ringing. Then your teacher will tell you to line up with no talking and follow him or her outside. It might be a little scary the first time you hear the bell ring, but it's a good idea to know what the sound means and what to do when you hear it in case there's ever a real fire.

Some days will be special. You may go to another room for gym class. Or you may visit the music room or the library. You may even go on a trip outside the school.

If it's a holiday or someone's birthday, your class
may even have a party!

All of the things you do in kindergarten and all of the special times throughout the year will be shared with the other children in your class. When you first come to school, you may not know anyone, and you may feel worried about this.

But soon you'll be playing and talking and laughing
with the boys and girls in your class.

And many of them will become your friends.

The other children aren't the only ones who will be your friends. Your teacher will be your best grown-up friend in school.

At the end of each day you will take your things
from your special place and get ready to go home.
Some days your teacher will give you papers to take
home. Some days you will take home the things
you've made to show your parents. They'll be very
happy to see the work you're doing in school. And
you'll feel proud of all the things you can do.

Your teacher will help you get to your bus or see
that you are picked up by whoever is walking home
with you.

And every day your classroom will be there after you've left, waiting for another day of kindergarten to begin.

James Howe was born and raised in New York State and received an M.A. degree in theater from Hunter College. While working as a literary agent for playwrights and other writers, Mr. Howe began writing himself. His first book for children, *Bunnicula: A Rabbit-Tale of Mystery* (an ALA Notable Book, winner of numerous state children's choice awards, and the subject of a network television special), was published in 1979. He has since written over a dozen more, including *The Day the Teacher Went Bananas* and *The Hospital Book* (an ALA Notable Book, American Book Award nominee, Boston Globe–Horn Book Honor Book, and SLJ Best Book of the Year).

Betsy Imershein grew up in New York and holds a master's degree in social work from Yeshiva University. She has been a social worker and psychotherapist and has worked as a free-lance producer for cable television. Ms. Imershein studied photography at the International Center of Photography, Parsons School of Design, and Cooper Union, and is particularly interested in documentary-style photography of children.

Mr. Howe and Ms. Imershein are married to each other and live in Hastings-on-Hudson, New York.